From Possum To Caviar

The Life and Times
of
Wiley Walter Virden

Written by Scott Graham and Wiley Virden

From Possum To Caviar

Life & Times of Wiley Walter Virden

Printed in the United States of America
Library of Congress Control Number: 2020916691

Author Scott Graham
Scott Graham holds
Electrical Engineering and Business Degrees from the Georgia Institute of Technology

He has worked in a myriad of fields including:

* Avionics on the F/A-18 Fighter for McDonnell Douglass
* Sold radar test equipment in the US and Europe for Scientific Atlanta
* Built 32 homes in the Atlanta Metro as owner of Graham Builders
* Worked in marketing, engineering and sales for Bell Labs (R&D development for AT&T)
* Sold backup power systems for Quality Standby Services
* Published author, public orator and member of Toast Masters
* As a historian, Scott has written numerous books dedicated to recording the history of people, places and events.
* He is an Eagle Scout and still spends time camping and hiking.

Scott enjoys golfing, sailing, surfing, fishing, swimming, skiing and working out.

Published by Scott Graham, Marietta, Georgia
wsgt@bellsouth.net - 404.431.2560
400 Lees Trace, Marietta, GA 30064

Design & Layout by Norm Cooper
Appalachian Books & Photography, Blairsville, Georgia

ISBN: 978-1-71659-582-0

This brief autobiography is written for my descendants and for those who come after me. From a reader's perspective, it may appear egotistical and it is meant to be. The purpose is to invite a look in my rearview mirror to learn what I am all about.

Wiley Virden

Atlanta - 1953

Early Life

On December 7, 1928, I was born in a share cropper's house, sired by a 58 year old father and a 32 year old mother. The Great Depression had begun, making it a poor way to start the race of life. My father, Walter Wiley Virden, had seven grown children, four sons and threes daughters when he lost his first wife. He then met my mother, Ophelia Stanfield. They fell in love and got married in 1924. From this marriage three siblings were born, Grace, Joy and myself.

My mother and her two wonderful sisters, Anice and Betty, were born on a tobacco farm in Tattnall County. Here parents were Lum Stanfield and Salie (Sally) Anderson. They were hard working, god fearing farmers and tough as nails. They lived off the land.

Early memories of my father have stayed with me all my life. Anywhere he went in his model-A four door convertible, I was standing by his side. Once, he took the family to see our first airplane. It was a "barnstormer", sitting in a pasture, the type Lindbergh flew in his early years.

In October of 1933, Dad left our home in Griffin with my mother's sister, Anice, to visit her other sister, Betty, in Reidsville, Georgia. I was to go with them. But at the last minute, for some reason I may never know, Mom changed her mind and kept me home. Dad never came back. Coming home by himself, he was forced off the road near Hawkinsville, Georgia by a drunk driver. The car came to rest upside down on top of dad and he was killed instantly.

News of the accident was on the front page of the Griffin News. It stated that he was one of the most respected men in Spalding County. This has given me great respect for him over the years.

After Dad's death, Mom was left with three children, very little education, no money and no way to make a living. Our entire world changed.

We moved into a small house a few blocks from downtown Griffin and mom took a job as a seamstress. Because downtown was my playground with little supervision, I inevitably found trouble. One day, I was accidently run over by Mrs. B. B. Brown in her car and my left leg was broken. A huge cast was placed on my leg that started at my thigh and went to my toes. Even though I was only five years old, I recall pushing it around on the floor for about four weeks.

I'll never forget Mom saying that we were invited to dinner at a friend's house for a possum dinner. Even at that early age, I knew something was wrong with that. As I look back, times were hard and people were hungry. We would eat almost anything.

During this time, Mom could only provide us with one meal a day, dinner. There was no money for breakfast or a lunch to take to school. I recall one afternoon when I was so hungry that I went to a neighbor's house and asked for a sandwich. They were kindly folks and gave me a sandwich along with a glass of milk. When Mom found out what I had done, she was upset. I'll never forget the look of pain and embarrassment on her face. I never did that again.

I imagine that it must have been heartbreaking for my mother not being able to provide birthday presents or Christmas gifts for her children. However, my mother may have given me a far greater gift because she gave me an intense desire to work hard and succeed.

Country Life

During my 7th year, Mom remarried. His name was Cliff Callaway, a farmer from South Georgia. He lived in a red house one mile from Mom's sister, Betty Tidwell in Tattnall County. Cliff had six children of his own, with four still living at home. This made a total of nine people living in a small five room house. Cliff was a good hard-working man, who raised me as if I was his own. At that time, the only way he knew to make a living was to farm.

My two sisters and I arrived in late fall, so off to school we went. Every day, we caught a bus with no heat or windows. Flaps kept the cold air out as much as possible. Hillview School had no electricity. The rooms were equipped with a single wood stove for heat. Each morning, the boys were tasked with scrounging enough firewood from the local woods to last for one day. The only light we had was from the windows. The school had a dirt basketball court and I always wanted to get in the game.

When spring came, country kids got out of school early to help on the farm. We all worked from sunup to sundown. We raised tobacco and cotton. We chopped cotton as it began to grow and picked it come September. We picked black berries and peaches for Mom to can for the winter. I'll never forget the smell of her cooking apples to can. It was wonderful.

Days on the farm weren't easy. My favorite time was the evenings when we would all gather to listen to the one radio we owned that ran on a battery. We could pick up WSB's 50,000 watt channel out of Atlanta. On hot nights we would all sit on the front porch and sing. We always had plenty of chickens to dress and hogs to slaughter on the cold mornings. Once a week, our clothes were washed in an old iron pot.

Share cropping didn't pay enough to stay there on the farm, and we moved back to Griffin in the fall. Jobs were hard to come by back then, but Cliff always found different jobs over the years.

Mom went back to work as a seamstress. Both incomes kept a roof over our heads and food on the table. We all pitched in, doing miscellaneous jobs, to bring a little extra money.

We didn't have much, but we were happy.

The Depression Years

School Patrol – Northside Grammar School, I'm on the far left

Growing up during the depression was tough. And because our family, friends and neighbors lived much the same way, we thought everyone lived as we did. We had very few clothes.

The winters were hard since we had no topcoats, but then again, neither did the other birds. The only heat in our home was a small pot-bellied stove. The warm mornings weren't so bad, but the bitter cold and rain that winter brought was a different ballgame.

Celebrations such as birthdays and Christmas were like any other day. Come Christmas, we might receive some fruit, but there was still no money for birthday gifts.

When Mom married Cliff, we ate better. I recall having oyster stew on Wednesday and fish on Friday. Sunday's dinner was special. We had fried chicken and for dessert we enjoyed Momma's delicious banana pudding.

There was no money to purchase items for personal hygiene such as toothbrushes. Sadly, false teeth were common in those days.

We had no toys in those days so we would manufacture our own, often making up "pretend" games. We flew homemade kites and made rubber guns from old inner tubes. We played baseball using a stick and a smashed tin can for a ball. Just about the only thing we had was each other.

When I turned twelve, I took a paper route delivering the Atlanta Constitution. Every day for two years, I awoke at four in the morning, folded and delivered my papers and then went directly to school. My salary was $2.50 a week of which half went toward payments for my Elgin bicycle.

There were good times and sad times. I can recall being unhappy as a child. I sometimes felt lost, looking for my father and the love that was missing from my life.

And then in the fourth grade my teacher, Ethel Goode, came into my life and paid special attention to me. I grew to love her. Fifty years later, I learned she was living in California and went to visit this wonderful woman in her home in Los Altos. The local paper sent a reporter to do a story on our reunion. The article along with our picture appeared on the front page. We stayed in touch until she passed away at the age of 84.

My early years were also filled with joyous memories. I'll never forget the three special summers I spent with my Aunt Betty, Uncle Lee and Cousins Russell and W. L. when I was 9, 10 and 11. The Tidwell's shared everything with me, treating me like a son and a brother, and I loved being a part of their family.

As tobacco farmers, they lived off the land, and I worked along beside them every day in the hot summer sun. The work was hard, but at the same time, it was gratifying. The only things they had to purchase were coffee, salt, pepper, flour, sugar and a few other items. Everything else, they grew or made themselves. I'll never forget the wonderful meals my Aunt Betty would make for us. We ate like kings. I loved the place. I came to appreciate the simple things, like sleeping under a tin roof during a rainstorm. To this day, when I hear rain on an unsupported tin roof, it always takes me back to those special summers and being a part of that loving family.

On that farm the stars and moon were like God had intended. I found comfort in the sounds of the farm animals, and the night birds off in the woods were music to my ears. I always looked forward to Saturday nights when we would gather in front of the radio, listening to the Grand Ol' Opry. I never dreamed that years later, I would spend the weekend with Minnie Pearl, the much-loved comedian, at her home in Nashville.

The Tidwell family is buried at the Old Anderson Church located in the country between Claxton and Collins, Georgia. My love for my Aunt Betty is still strong. Her love for me has comforted me when I had needed it most. If I had roots, they were there. The country stills beckons me, and to this day, I never go to the coast without going out to see the old home place and to my Aunt's grave.

A fond memory from my second marriage was when Tootsie and I were there in August of 1978. We went to the "swimming hole" on Cedar Creek and went skinny dipping where I swam as a young boy.

Despite missing my Mom, Cliff and brothers and sisters, it was a sad day at the end of those special summers when a car would come down the lane to take me home to Griffin. Bless you, Aunt Betty!

High School and Athletics

Halfback at Darlington School, 1947-48

As a young boy growing up, I wanted to join in on any kind of sporting events. Touch football every Saturday morning, grammar school basketball, baseball… you name it. I was there. I loved to compete.

During my high school years, I played football, basketball and ran track. If we had a baseball team, I would have played that as well. I was not exposed to tennis or golf at that point. My best sport was track. I ran the dashes, relays, threw the discus and javelin. I won the state discus championships my first three years in high school. My senior year, I won the mid-south regional, held at the Georgia Tech field, and established a discus state record that was not broken until a few years ago.

Football was my ticket to Darlington School, a private prep school located in Rome, Georgia where I spent my final two years of high school. I not only played four years in high school.

I also played one year at the University of Florida and service ball in Japan during the Korean War.

Later in life, I took up tennis and golf. I became a B-plus tennis player and a four handicapper in golf at the age of fifty-two. I have had two hole-in-ones and 26 eagles. The lowest score I ever shot was a seventy. Over the years, I have played great golf courses including the Augusta National and Pebble Beach. My two trips to Ireland to play golf with friends were also great experiences. Additionally, in the 90s I played in Dominican Republic at Casa De Campo five straight years. At the age of eighty-four, I still enjoy golf.

In the summer of 1945, I was wearing a pair of blue jeans and thumbing a ride to the local park for a swim with 25 cents and a towel. A nice car stopped, carrying two friendly looking ladies in the front seat. When I jumped in the back seat, I came face to face with a cutest blond, blue-eyed girl I had ever laid eyes on. I was in love. Her name was Carolyn Bramblett. At that moment, I had no idea just how much she would influence my life. I loved her for many years and she gave me wonderful memories that I will always cherish.

In May of 1946, I walked to Jessie's Pharmacy in downtown Griffin. As teenagers, we would hang out there, enjoying our cokes. On this particular evening, three friends asked me to join them on a trip to Barnesville to attend the graduation exercises at Gordon Military College. I was all set to go when my close friend, Earl Rowe, came in and talked me into going elsewhere with him. Within 30 minutes, the boys headed to Barnesville were in a terrible car wreck. Two were killed and the third spent his life in a wheelchair.

Darlington School

Darlington School was my salvation. It was one of the most prestigious boys' schools in the south. Darlington was a military school with no military. It had dress codes, inspections and rigid rules to follow. Teachers called students mister and students did the same for teachers. We used nicknames for all our teachers, but never to their face. Honesty, integrity, etiquette and being true to one's self were stressed. Social manners and interacting with people were also a part of our maturation. Sons of prominent families attended. Some young men were there for disciplinary reasons.

The teachers were the best that could be found. They were feared and loved from the president on down. They understood that boys reacted to hard work and challenges.

Football paved the way for my acceptance to Darlington. They were part of the Mid-South Conference and could recruit and play post grades. It was similar to a college freshman team. Despite my weak scholastic record, they needed a half-back and I was admitted. The teachers had an uphill battle to get me through.

I left behind Griffin High School and that bad environment to find myself in a shocking, new world. I soon found myself being molded and polished into someone my family and I could be proud of. It wasn't long before I began to meet and date some of the prettiest girls in Rome and Atlanta.

My half brother, John, who made it possible for me to attend Darlington, always came out to watch the athletic events during both my years there. We both filled a void for one another. He found a son in me and I found a dad in him. I felt an immense sense of pride every time I looked to the sideline and saw him smoking his cigar and cheering me on. On john's death bed, he told me those years were the happiest of his life.

Most of my friends today are old Darlington boys. Through Darlington, I came to know some of the finest men in the world. I was very fortunate to have been a part of that wonderful school—bless you John.

Last game of the year, Thanksgiving 1947 against Tennessee Military Institute Dick Pretz Jr., "Footsie" Wallace, Tommy Kirkland and Wiley

A Special Weekend in New Orleans

In 1949, I was attending the University of Florida. During the Christmas Holidays, I joined my brother and few of his friends on a trip to New Orleans to attend the Sugar Bowl and the horse races. We boarded a train in Newnan, Georgia for the all-night trip. While working our way to the Pullman car, I passed one of the prettiest girls I had ever seen. I came back to look for her, but she had retired for the night. The next morning, I met her in the dinning car where she told me her name, Patsy Doubleday. She was on her way to Harlingen, Texas to visit her mother, who didn't know she was coming. To make a long story short, I talked her into staying over the weekend in New Orleans. During our weekend together, I fell in love with Patsy.

In February, I decided to visit her during the weeklong break between Semesters. My finances were tight and I planned to hitchhike all the way. After class on Friday, I hit the road with my large suitcase. It had a large Florida Gator on it, marking me as a college student, so I had no trouble catching rides. Looking back, I cannot believe that I left behind thousands of coeds to see one girl a million miles away.

I arrived in New Orleans at night and took a bus out to the highway going to Texas. When I arrived in Houston, I telephoned a relative and then headed south. I caught a ride with a tractor trailer truck to Corpus Christy and arrived there at three AM on Sunday. I took a bus the rest of the way. Once in Harlingen, I called Patsy. She and her mother came to pick me up. Patsy and I were together for the next four days, four wonderful days.

Thursday morning, I was on the road, headed for Houston. I was completely out of money. The weather turned cold and I didn't have enough warm clothes, standing with the wind cutting through me. I made it to Houston and spent the night with my relative. The next morning, I was on the road to Beaumont when I was picked up by a gay guy who put the move on me. I got out at the next town.

I was standing at the end of a bridge next to my big gator suitcase, freezing. I then spotted a convertible crossing the bridge with Texas plates. When it stopped, I ran to the window and asked, "How far are you going?"

The driver smiled and said, "How far do you think we're going? We're

My Family

Mrs. Salie Stanfield with daughters from left to right: Ophelia (Virden) Griffin GA; Betty (Tidwell) Manassas, GA; Anice (Holland) Forest City, NC

Regardless of any success I may have accomplished, I never deserted my family. I was never ashamed of where I came from nor embarrassed by any member with few exceptions. I just love them knowing we are all God's children. I have always helped them in time of need. There were times when some needed financial aid. I would never loan them money. I just gave it to them and was happy that I was able to help. I have never looked down on uneducated or low-income folks nor looked up to the wealthy. One member of my family referred to me as, "our lovable rich uncle".

I love the story about a man in Chicago, who was able to step out of the dark shadow left by his father. He grew into a fine man in the late 30's. The war came and he became a fighter pilot in the Pacific. For his actions, he was awarded the Medal of Honor. In fact, the city named an airport in his honor. His name was O'Hare. His father was a hit man for Al Capone.

My Mother

From the time I left home, I never forgot my mother. When I came to live in another world, and whatever accomplishments I may have achieved, I was there for her. When she wanted to visit friends or family or to take a trip, I was the one who took her. Losing her husband at a young age and left to raise a family on her own must have been difficult. Still, I never heard her complain and she always had an upbeat, positive attitude. No matter how bad things were, she always smiled and was a joy to be around. She instilled these qualities in her children and I will always be grateful.

In the 70s, she went on her first and only airplane ride. She would only fly with her grandson, David. Their picture appeared in the Griffin News.

My Mother's Family

Lum Stanfield

19

My mother, Ophelia Stanfield, was born in 1902 and died in her sleep in 1981. She now rests in the family cemetery at the County Line Church in Digby, GA. Digby is a crossroad out from Griffin where I was born. Her father was Lum Stanfield and her mother was Salie Anderson.

The Andersons migrated to Georgia from North Carolina in the mid 1800s. They settled in Tattnall County. The county seat was Glenville. They were farmers. My great-great-grandfather was a primitive Baptist and founded the old Anderson Church located between Collins and Claxton. Many of my ancestors are buried there including Aunt Betty and her family. Mother's family had no formal education, but were great farmers and were honest, religious, hard working people.

Not much is known about the Stanfields. Mom's uncle was Jim Stanfield and I later came to know an Atlanta lawyer by the same name. By some strange coincidence, he turned out to be Jim's son and my cousin. Some years later, a friend from Claxton told me about a settlement of Stanfields in the Claxton area.

Over the years, mother entertained me with stories about life in the late 1800s and early 1900s. Her grandfather owned a great deal of land and when one of his children married, he would give them a few acres to build a home and begin a life of their own with their children. He also delivered mail in a buggy. He loved to stop and visit with the local farmers and talk politics. Mother said that he carried a whip and would crack the whip to start his horse. He was a true Georgia cracker.

About the time my favorite aunt, Aunt Betty, married Lee Tidwell, Mom and Anice sold their land and moved to Barnesville where they met their future husbands, Wiley Virden and CM Holland.

Aunt Betty and Lee had four children: W. L., Russell, Dorothy and a child who died at the age of four. Dorothy killed herself in 1934 at the age of 16 after her father would not let her date an older man.

CM was from Forest City, NC and Aunt Anice joined him there until her death. He ran a small barber shop in Alexander Mills Station, just outside Forest City. The little building is still there. Their son, Monroe, was like a brother to me. He died in 1994. If you are ever in the area, you should look up descendants of the Holland family.

My Father's Family

I can trace my father's family back to 1791. Eginear Virden married a girl by the name of Winny in Upson County in 1841. They had a son, William, who married Elizabeth Gordon. One of their sons, Samuel, married Laura Pritchett. One of their sons, Walter Virden, my father, married Ida Elizabeth White. Walter, born in 1869, was killed in an automobile wreck in 1933. As mentioned, they had seven children: Ella, Eda, Harvey, John, Jesse, Walter and Minnie Ruth. There was another child, but little is known of him.

Following the death of Ida, my father remarried Ophelia Stanfield, my mother. She had three more children, my two older sisters, Grace and Joy, and me. When my father was killed in the auto accident, mother remarried Cliff Calloway who had six children of his own: Wilton, Hazel, Wallace, Grace, Amy and Ellis. From this marriage, two more children were born: Clyde and Nancy. Clyde married Jackie and they had one daughter, Carmille. Carmille married Reverend Kenny Thompson. They have two siblings, Caroline and Zack, and reside in Newnan, Georgia. Nancy married Robert Dorton and had four children: Mandy, Lynn, David and Mitchell.

Phillip Stewart

Philip was my second cousin's youngest son. At a young age, he contracted cerebral palsy and spent his entire life in a wheelchair. Sadly, very few members of our family spent time with him or tried to make his life more pleasant. However, I saw a heart of gold in this young man and loved to be around him. He inspired me and I always tried to show him my appreciation.

During my life, I made many trips to Griffin. Most of the time, Phillip was on my list of people to see. He was an avid Georgia Bulldog fan and I pulled for Tech. We had fun going at each other. One Thanksgiving, I surprised him by introducing him to Coach Dooley. We went to a local motel the day before the Tech versus Georgia game, and Coach Dooley spent 30 minutes with Phillip. I cannot describe the delight I felt when Phillip's face lit up once he realized the surprise. That was the year I pulled for Georgia to win the game.

Phillip loved golf. He joined me on one of my rounds of golf at the Griffin course and we had a great time. I acquired pictures and autographs from his two favorite golfers, Sam Snead and Jack Nickolas. I also arranged for his first and only airplane ride.

One summer day, I stopped by for a short visit. The house was like an oven. I could not help but notice that he was perspiring in his leather wheelchair. I was upset to learn that their little home had no air conditioning. I called his brother, Dee, and three days later, Phillip was enjoying cool air. Phillip was very grateful, but his brothers never thanked me.

I would like to point out that my son David also took an interest in Phillip. He spent time and money to provide Phillip with a computer and to keep it running.

I like to think that God was also involved. We lost Phillip when God took him while he slept. I like to think that I will see Phillip's smiling face again, someday.

My Atlanta Family

When I first arrived in Atlanta, I had no money, nor family. I had a few friends from my Darlington days who lived in Atlanta, one being Dick Pretz. Dick and I remained close friends for life. He and his family took me in as one of their own. His mother became my Atlanta mother. She was one of the truly great ladies of her time. She taught me many things including etiquette, how to dress and interact with people. She was a woman with great wisdom and shared some of it with me. She helped me become a gentleman, and I often look back on the advice she offered, amazed at how much it changed my life for the better.

She was a patron of the arts and introduced me to the great music of the world. Her advice concerning how to treat women was most enlightening. Under her guidance, I became comfortable in the social and business world. She also taught me the importance of sharing my wisdom and helping others as she had helped me. I will always be indebted to this woman who I came to love as a second mother.

My Marriages and Children

My first marriage was to Mary (Gini) Virginia Fowler, in June of 1954. We had two children: Laura, born on March 10, 1955 and David, born on March 19, 1956. Laura gave us three grandchildren: Corey McMillan, born on November 15, 1990, Cody McMillan, born on November 24, 1995 and Chris McMillan, born on Sept 27, 1989.

Sad to say, Laura betrayed my trust and David abandoned me. However, I had many loving, caring family members who were a special part of my life.

My second marriage was to Margret (Tootsie) Strain, on June 5, 1974. Tootsie's son from a previous marriage is Andrew C. Robinson, Jr.

My third marriage was to Kaye Banner Graham on September 21, 1985. Kaye's son from a previous marriage is Scott Graham. Kaye's daughter is Melissa Ermutlu.

Gini and Wiley – 1955

Korea
1950 – 1952

Camp Poke - 1950

After a year at the University of Florida, I realized that I was not yet ready for college. Not only did I need more basic education, I needed to grow up and become more mature. Joining the military and serving my country was the ticket.

While visiting friends in Detroit, Michigan, I enlisted in the army for a two-year hitch. Enlistees were sent to Fort Ord in Chicago and then on to Camp Poke in Louisiana. We were "fill-ins" for the 45th Infantry Division out of Oklahoma. This was Oklahoma's National Guard. After basic training in a bitterly cold winter, we embarked in New Orleans for a 30-day voyage to Hokkaido, Japan.

Advanced training was in order for the next three months. In December, the division was shipped to Korea, relieving the First Calvary Division on New Years Eve of 1951. We served on the front lines for the next nine months. I was promoted to the rank of Master Sargent. During this time, I was awarded the Silver Star for my participation in the Battle of T-bone Hill. I returned home in October of 1952.

Award of the Silver Star

The following citation was awarded on July 6, 1952:

Sergeant First Class Wiley W. Virden, Jr., RA1634512, Infantry, United States Army, Company I, 179th Infantry Regiment, 45th Infantry Division, distinguished himself by gallantry in action against an armed enemy near Karhyonni, Korea. Company I was entrenched in defensive positions on Hill 191, T-bone Hill, on the night of 15 June 1952 in anticipation of enemy counterattacks. An initial barrage of more than five thousand hostile mortar and artillery shells fell on the regiment. When a company sized attack was launched at Sergeant Virden's platoon, he unhesitatingly left the cover of his trench to direct furious counter-fire on the onrushing enemy troops. Even during the most intense action, Sergeant Virden remained in an entirely exposed area in order to control the defensive fire and to combat the enemy with rifle fire and hand grenades. So inspirational was Sergeant Virden's example and leadership that in spite of the overwhelming numbers of the attackers, the enemy was repulsed with heavy casualties. Sergeant Virden's gallantry in the face of great odds reflects the highest credit on himself and the United Sates Army. Sergeant Virden entered the Federal service from Georgia.

The night of June 15th, there were roughly 130 men and myself that were tasked with holding T-bone Hill, a Chinese held hill on the main battle line. Our company was dug in on a knoll with the Chinese looking down on us. We knew they would attack and completely surround us. The sun set and it wasn't long before we found ourselves being shelled by the enemy with nothing but trenches for protection. After 30 minutes of hell, the shelling ceased. The attack followed. When daylight came, only 23 of us walked off the hill. It was the worst night of my life. I lost many close friends, some of the finest men in this world who would never return home despite having families to raise and loved ones to care for.

Division Level Football

The 45th infantry had a division level football team. They needed 10 players to complete the team. I tried out and joined them. During September, October and November, we traveled to five major Japanese cities, playing against Air Force teams. We were to play in the Rice Bowl in Tokyo, but it was cancelled when we were ordered back to Korea in December.

Camp Poke, boot camp - 1950
Company I Squad (Wiley top row, 2nd from left)

Final Night on the Front Lines

Three days before we were to be relieved and I could go home, our company was ordered to defend the top of "Ol' Baldy", a hill where many battles had been fought. It was shaped like a man's skull and all the vegetation had been blown away, leaving only stumps.

The first two nights were quiet. At eight PM on the last night I was in the command post and answered a call from one of our company commanders.

"Intelligence tells us the Chinese plan an attack at 10 PM," he said. "Be ready; this attack could hit 'Ol' Baldy'."

I notified the squad leaders in the trenches and we waited. Many thoughts went through my mind. I somehow survived T-Bone Hill. Could I survive another barrage? Would I die on my last night in Korea?

At precisely 10 PM we heard the artillery go off and knew the rounds were headed our way. My eyes were filled with tears when we realized the shells all dropped two miles away.

Our relief, young green soldiers who had never been in combat, arrived at four AM. Most were killed the following night when the Chinese attacked Ol' Baldy.

We marched to our awaiting trucks. When I climbed into the cab, the driver smiled and said, "You are going home."

Marion Galbreath and Wiley digging fox hole
Hokkaido, Japan - 1951

Friends, Business and the Social World

Griffin
1948

Griffin had a Class D baseball league that year. The commissioner of baseball, "Happy" Chandler, came to Griffin to visit the team. I was a friend of Dan, his son. I attended the game and "Happy" insisted that I sit with him. I watched the entire game sitting between "Happy" and the Governor of Georgia, M. E. Thomson. It was a big night for a boy from Digby, Georgia.

The Debutante Ball
Christmas 1953

Following my time in the US Army, I arrived in Atlanta to return to college and contacted Richard Wilson, an old Darlington School friend. He invited me to my first social event, his sister's wedding. Another Darlington School friend, Dick Pretz, was also in attendance. Dick was my running mate in track and football at Darlington. He was still playing football for Georgia Tech under the revered coach, Bobby Dodd. These two close friends took me to the water and I drank.

Through one of Dick's teammates, I met Susan Hull, a beauty from one of Atlanta's finest families. She was an officer in the Debutante Club. After a few dates, she invited me to be her escort when she made her debut. The affair was held at the prestigious Piedmont Driving Club. I'm not sure her family was too excited about her choice of an escort, but we got along. They probably suspected that I didn't know what a Debutante was and they weren't far from the truth. Bill Van Thaden, another Tech football player, and I double dated and off we went to one of the most festive night of our lives. It was attended by families, guests and fifty of Atlanta's most eligible women.

Little did I know that I would meet Gini Fowler, my future wife and mother of my children. Many photos were snapped and Susan and I appeared on the society page of the Atlanta news paper. It was a great affair, one that I'll never forget, and marked the beginning of my social life in Atlanta. Five years before, I didn't even know how to hold a dinner fork properly. Thank you, Darlington School!

An Important Man

I am a longtime friend of Jack O'Guy, Jr., who was from Claxton, Georgia. Jack was George Bush's wing man in the South Pacific during the war. He was awarded the Navy Cross and the Distinguished Flying Medal. Jack arranged to have President Bush and his wife Barbara come to Claxton a few years before Jack passed away.

The Business and Social World

In the business world, one must have the ability to perform and follow through with promises. With that, who you know plays a large part in becoming successful. A great example of this is what happened to my son David. He had five years of Air Control experience. When he applied to the FAA, they would not hire him because he was not the right color. I told him to sit tight and made one phone call. The next day, Senator Sam Nunn made a personal telephone call to David. In two weeks, David was working in the tower at the airport for the FAA. He had a distinguished career with them and is now retired.

I entered the insurance business when my chances of success were nil and none. Getting to know the right people and being at the right place at the right time went a long way toward my success. In the 70s I only had two agents, Mr. Johnson and Mr. Bryan. Over the years, the road has been bumpy, but I made it. Today, my little company, Johnson and Bryan, has 90 employees and writes over 140 million dollars in business. We were chosen in the top ten property and casualty insurance agencies in Atlanta by the Atlanta Business Chronicle, Atlanta's top business magazine.

Socially, I have lived a good life. Being a member of the Cherokee Country

Club and the County Club of Sapphire Valley, I have gotten to know many successful people. These clubs have provided a great social life that I would not have had if I were not a member.

Life at Cherokee Country Club
1968 – 2013

With the financial help of Gini's parents, we joined the Cherokee Town and Country Club. I was a member of the Castle View Club, but it went bankrupt in 1965. Cherokee purchased the beautiful Grant home on West Paces Ferry Road, making this their clubhouse. Tommy Tillman, a neighbor, sponsored us. The president, Bob Holder, also a friend who lived near by, pushed our membership, and we were accepted in a short period of time.

I already knew some of the members due to my association with the Atlanta Jaycees and the Wieuca Road Baptist Church. Being a golfer and tennis player, I quickly met and became close friends with many of the members. Quite a few of my Cherokee friends became business customers and I still handle their insurance accounts today. There is a saying that I agree with: "never marry for money, just marry where money is".

Over the years, I served on many committees: membership, finance, tennis and golf, to name a few. In 2005, Cherokee was named the number one country club in America. Without a doubt, being a part of Cherokee was of great value, adding to my business and social life. Our members were the elite in the business and social world of Atlanta.

Life in the Atlanta Junior Chamber of Commerce

The Atlanta Jaycees was a great steppingstone to the business and social world of Atlanta. Any young businessman, who wanted to succeed, joined the Jaycees. It was a great training ground for young men. Here I learned about politics, public speaking and civic affairs.

I served six years on their board of directors but was never elected as an officer. I became co-chairman of the 1961 National Convention held in Atlanta. Fifteen thousand members converged on Atlanta for three days.

For two years, doors were open to me that otherwise would have been closed. I was able to attend lunch in the Board Room of directors of Coca Cola. During this period, I met and worked with Mayor Hartsfield to dedicate the Merchandise Mart and to promote Atlanta. It was during this time that my name appeared on the front page of the Atlanta Journal. The article was about a verbal battle I had with Governor Rockefeller over whether or not to allow the New York Jaycees to wear Union Civil War uniforms in the south. They did and it was lots of fun watching the Mississippi Jaycees dressed in grey fight a mock reenactment battle against the New Yorkers that was held at Kennesaw Mountain.

My wife, Gini, was in charge of the ladies' program and did a wonderful job. Two close friends came to me through the Jaycees; DeJon Franklin and Clifford Oxford, both prominent Atlanta attorneys.

Perhaps one of my favorite memories occurred just before the Jaycee parade in downtown Atlanta. During a sudden rain, I found myself under an umbrella along with three Miss Americas. My time with the Jaycees were wonderful days!

My Weekend with Minnie Pearl

Not long after my divorce from my first wife Gini, I met Bunny Muller, a wonderful, fun loving and athletic young woman who was an avid tennis player. She asked me to join her for a weekend in Nashville to play in the Charlotte-Pearl Tennis Tournament. This was a top social event put on by Minnie Pearl, the Grand Old Opera star and comedienne. We were to stay in her home. Of course, I accepted. I had listened to and laughed with Minnie since I was a kid.

We drove to Nashville on Friday afternoon and soon arrived at Minnie's home. She lived on a beautiful estate next door to the governor of Tennessee, Winfield Dunn. We rang the doorbell and were greeted by Minnie. "Minnie, this is Wiley," said Bunny. Minnie flashed that famous grin of hers when she met a handsome young man. "Now Minnie, you leave him alone."

Minnie looked at me and said, "You know, Wiley, there are a lot of things worse than sleeping with a 60-year-old woman." That was the beginning of a wonderful and unforgettable weekend.

After the tournament late Saturday, we gathered in Minnie's pool house. She played the piano and sang until the late hours. On Sunday morning, Governor Dunn come over and we played doubles tennis. I was Minnie's partner and we won.

Driving home, I told Bunny I wished I could have taken pictures. I didn't think it was the thing to do. Bunny laughed and said I could have taken all the pictures I wanted. I was so sad that I had missed the chance. Bunny also told me that Burt Reynolds and Dianna Shore had left Minnie's guest house the day before we arrived.

When Minnie passed away, I called Bunny and we both shed a few tears.

My Life With Young People

Loving the game of football and being around kids, I officiated high school football for eight years. The experience made me want to return to my years on the gridiron.

In the sixties, I joined the Big Brother program. We were working with boys with no male image in their homes. Not until my older stepbrother, John, stepped into my life, did I have a real father figure. I understand the importance of a father figure and wanted to help these young men. Over the years, I had four little brothers. Helping these boys gave me a great deal of happiness. I served on their Atlanta Board of Directors for two years.

Also in the sixties, I started a class for boys in our mission church on Ashby Street in southwest Atlanta. I began with two boys, one black and one white, the minister's son. I built the class to fifteen boys in our first year. We formed a basketball team and played in a church league. One summer, I raised enough money to send them to a summer camp.

For almost a decade, I taught twelve-year-old boys in Sunday school at the Wieuca Baptist Church. I bonded with these boys and word got around that my class was the one to be in. Over the years, I've been approached by young men who remembered being in my classes. This, too, has given me a great satisfaction.

For two years, I taught a co-ed class of 21 to 29-year-old singles. The major subject was "How to Mix Religion in the Business World". This was very interesting to them, having to live in a secular world. Their feedback changed my thinking on many issues.

Having joined the Peachtree-Atlanta Kiwanis Club in 1968, I was appointed the chairmanship of the Boys and Girls Committee. I was asked to come up with a project that would promote scholastic achievement. The end result was the beginning of the "Student Improvement Award" in the Atlanta

School System. The teachers would select a girl and boy from each class who had made the most improvement during the year. The improvement could be in grades, deportment or anything deserving recognition.

This project spread to the Fulton County and Floyd County schools and is still in practice today. Since 1968, thousands of young lives have been brightened by the recognition this program has brought. This has given me a good deal of satisfaction.

Religion And Seeking the Truth

At the age of 36, I began to make a comprehensive study of the Bible. After a two-year study of the most interesting book I've ever read, I had many questions. In search of answers, I read numerous books about all the major religions of the world. It was a real education. But it wasn't until I read The History of God, written by a former Catholic nun, that many of my questions were answered.

My personal belief about religion is this: believe in Christ, live a good life, do your duty and a crown will be waiting. In my early 30's, I became obsessed with educating myself. As a hobby, I began to read biographies. That in itself is an education. True history can only be found in the lives of great people. Following my study of the world's great religions, I was amazed at what I found.

As I sought the truth, a secret history began to unfold, a history not made public nor taught in our schools. I found this to be true as I began my study of the races of people. The greatest lies in history came before my eyes. In my study of conflicts between nations, I found that the masses were often ignorant as to why they fought. The victors write the history and only one side is revealed in history books.

The more educated I became; the more I sought the truth. The bible says, "For those who seek the truth, much grief will follow." Another truism comes to mind. "Those who seek the truth walk a lonely road." I wanted to know both sides of any major issue. I read many books that can't be bought in most bookstores. Most people only know what they read in the news and see on television and movies. In most cases, that is all they want to know. Truth and the American media are foreign to each other.

As I shared what I learned with friends, I became a person to avoid. "Don't discuss events with him," became the message. I've found other truth-seekers who share my views, but more often than not, I walk alone.

Speeches of Note

In the sixties, I taught class of black boys at a mission church in southwest Atlanta. The sole reason for my involvement was to help the boys. However, after my experience, I realized that I enjoyed speaking to groups, especially when speaking about subjects that were near and dear to my heart.

Kiwanis
1972

In 1972, I was Lt. Governor of the first district of Kiwanis. I received a telephone call asking me to be the keynote speaker at one of their luncheons. I accepted. This was the downtown Atlanta club, the largest in the state. My wife's father and brother were members. At noon on the appointed date, I spoke to over 200 of Atlanta's top businessmen. Students from Circle-K and the K-club were in attendance. At the conclusion, I received a standing ovation. It was a memorable moment for me. I was told by the chapter president, "They don't stand up for many people."

Darlington School Speech
1974

One cold, wet day after a weekend visit, I drove my son David back to Darlington School after a weekend visit. I noticed the American flag hanging in the rain. The flag was old, weathered and torn. I found this sight disturbing and wrote the dean, offering to donate a new flag if he would allow me to speak to the students about patriotism. He was grateful and invited me to address all 250 students. Following my impassioned speech, the boys stood, cheered and gave me a standing ovation that lasted a full three minutes, leaving me with tears in my eyes. I then presented the student body president with a new flag. I still meet young men, who were in attendance and remember that special speech.

Marquis De Lafayette

Being an avid reader of biographies, I enjoyed the life of Lafayette more than any other. Charles Lindbergh was a close second (Lindbergh was not a pro-Nazi; he was one of America's greatest heroes). When asked to speak to my Buckhead Kiwanis Club at a regular noon meeting, I chose to speak about Lafayette. A few visiting Kiwanis members asked if I would come to their chapters and give the same speech. At that time, I didn't imagine that I would give this speech more than 30 times. I spoke at Rotary Clubs, Garden Clubs and the Sons of the American Revolution. One memorable talk on Lafayette took place in my hometown. I spoke to the Griffin Kiwanis Club and a picture was taken of the club president and me. The local paper published the picture, making me very proud.

Gordon College

In the eighties, I was asked to address a group of 150 business students at Gordon College in Barnesville, Georgia. The subject was "What Is It Like in the Business World". My speech was well received, so much so that they requested me to come back two additional years.

Highlights in My Life

- Returning from Korea aboard a troop ship in 1952 and watching 1700 men burst into tears when the Golden Gate Bridge came into view.
- Being awarded the Silver Star by a General in the field in Korea.
- Introducing my friend, Dr. Noah Langdale, the president of Georgia State University, to my Northside Kiwanis Club.
- Having a conversation with Mr. John Portman, the internationally known architect, in his home at Sea Island, Georgia.
- Escorting a lovely lady to a dance at Sea Island. She was worth two hundred million dollars.
- Dedicating the downtown Atlanta Merchandise Mart with Mayor Hartsfield in 1961.
- A romantic lunch date with Gwen Verdon, the famous star of Broadway in the 40s and 50s.
- Dinner with Jonathon Winters in St. Louis in 1960. He was a much-loved comedian in movies and television.
- Dinner at Cherokee Country Club with Joan Southerland, the internationally known Opera star.
- Having many people tell me that I resembled Arnold Palmer and Jack Nicholas (in looks only).
- Being awarded the "Hixon Award", the highest honor bestowed by Kiwanis International.
- Sitting on the front row, enjoying the great Italian operatic tenor, Luciano Pavoratti, perform.
- Twice attending the Kentucky Derby
- Seeing my grandsons
- Running for a fifty-yard touchdown in Tokyo, Japan with General Mathew Ridgeway in attendance
- My first hole-in-one in January 2000
- Attending the Masters Golf Tournament for twenty-one years
- Three Miss Americas and me under my umbrella during a light rain in 1961
- Having my dad for four years

- Spending a weekend in the home of Minnie Pearl, the country comedian of the Grand Ol' Opry in Nashville.
- In 1950, I was made a "Kentucky Colonel" by Governor "Happy" Chandler, one of the few who lived outside the state
- Playing a round of golf with Atlanta's former mayor, Ivan Allen Jr., in Sapphire Valley
- My wife and I were in the VIP section at the launching of Apollo 13. Gini was a friend of Fred Haise's wife. Fred was kind enough to give Gini a personal tour of the center in Houston. Later, I had lunch with Fred in Detroit while attending a national Kiwanis Convention. Fred was one of the three astronauts featured in the film, Apollo 13.
- Rooming next to and being on a New York City elevator with Joe DiMaggio, the great baseball player and husband of Maryland Monroe
- Winning first flight in golf at Cherokee Country Club with rounds of 78, 76 and 75 in 1977
- Burning down the old football stadium in Griffin in 1945
- Playing Augusta National golf course in 1978
- Writing a golf novel, Center Stage in Jodeco
- A visit to California to see my favorite grade schoolteacher, who taught fourth grade, fifty years later
- Playing Pebble Beach golf course three times
- Being baptized in 40-degree water in Japan
- Meeting Slim Pickens, the movie star, at Forest Fowler's home in 1968
- Given a personal tour of Lexington, Kentucky horse farms by Mimi Chandler, daughter of Happy Chandler, Governor of Kentucky
- Attending the Army vs Penn State football game at West Point in 1959
- Playing and beating Athens High School in a 1945 football game held at the University of Georgia, Sanford Stadium
- Enjoying my son's success as an air traffic controller
- Having two holes-in-one and twenty-six Eagles
- Becoming president of my company at the age of 39
- Taking my first commercial airline flight to New Orleans in 1947
- Elected president of the Atlanta Area Football Officials Association in 1958
- Going through the Panama Canal in 1950

Kind Words and Honest Observations From Friends and Acquaintances

"Wiley, you missed your calling. You should have worked with boys. They bond quicker with you than with any person I've known."
Richard Henshaw
A close friend

"The problem with you is, you don't know your own potential."
Patsy Hubert
Girlfriend – 1953

"Wiley, if it wasn't for your poor attitude, you could be an All American."
University of Florida football coach – 1950

"Wiley, you don't realize what you have accomplished in life."
Phil Osborne
Osborne Travel
Darlington classmate – 1992

"Of all the boys I've taught at Darlington, Wiley Virden surprised me more than any other."
Walter Judd
Darlington professor

"Wiley, when you came to Darlington, you were just a lump of coal. You needed a lot of polish."
Mr. J. P. King
Darlington Professor

"Wiley, your 102-yard run against Notre Dame prep was the greatest I've ever seen in football."
Mr. Richard Pretz, Sr.
Georgia Tech professor

"You were the best Lt. Governor the Georgia Kiwanis ever had."
Dave Kunckler
President of the Peachtree Atlanta Kiwanis Club

"You have more athletic ability than any player I've coached in a long time."
Coach Jim Cavan
Griffin High School

"That was the best speech we have heard at our club in a long time."
Joe Zigler
President of the Atlanta Kiwanis Club

"I don't know of anyone in the Cherokee Club that doesn't like you."
Tom Tollison
Member

"You are one of the last of the good ol' country boys."
Emmett McDowell
Close friend

"I would trust Wiley with anything I have."
Mr. H. H. Hunt, CPA, to Carolyn Wynn
1962

"Wiley loved and looked after his family."
Jenette Virden

"We are all proud of you. I am a better man because of knowing you."
Scott Gregory
VP Johnson and Bryan
"You are educated beyond your intelligence."
Mrs. Richard Pretz
1965

"Your maturity was trailing your intelligence at a considerable distance."
John B. Virden, brother
First year at University of Florida

"You are very impulsive."
Lelia Virden
Sister-in-Law

"Wiley, don't go into politics—you are too honest."
Bill Callaway
1973

"You are a wonderful man and you make me very happy."
D. D. Petters
2001

"You are an amazing man, Wiley Virden. Your friends are a testament to a life well lived and greatly enjoyed."
Gail Jackson
Harry Norman Realty
2002

"Wiley, I know of no one who has more entertaining stories, jokes and witticisms than you. You have a gift for making people smile, even strangers."
Scott Graham
Stepson

"Your book, Center Stage in Jodeco, was one of the best golf stories I have read. It would make a great movie."
Phil Mouchet
The Mouchet Corporation
Griffin, Georgia

"Wiley, you can be the state Kiwanis Governor if you want it."
Early Williams
Buckhead Kiwanis

"You are the best detail man I ever knew."
O. K. Sheffield
Fulton National Bank
Jaycee National Convention

"I've never seen you with an unattractive woman."
Fred Cassel, Jr.
Houston, Texas
2003

"Wiley, you're not old—never will be. You're a guy who started with nothing and built yourself up by your bootstraps. I admire you."
Ed Simmons
An old friend

Best Advice: "Every time I lost my temper, I lost!"
Father-in-law's friend who was president and owner of an Atlanta auto dealership

Goodbye to Sapphire Valley

In July of 1977, my second wife Tootsie and I moved into our second home in Cashiers, North Carolina. We joined the Country Club of Sapphire Valley. I've been there for 36 wonderful years, making great memories with family, friends and neighbors.

At the age of 85, I felt it was time for me to move on. Sapphire Valley is a magical place and it was with a heavy heart that I submitted a letter of resignation to the Country Club. At the same time, I wrote a poem that I shared with my friends who had been a part of my life there. The response was overwhelming—they loved it. I wanted to end my story with my poem and hope you enjoy it as well.

My Heaven
By Wiley Virden

As the light of my life faded into eternal darkness,
An angel was waiting to take my hand and lead me to the promise land.

In an instant, I stood before the throne of God,
His hair was as white as a winter snow,
His voice flowed as gentile as the breeze on a summer night.

"My son, you have believed in me; you've stayed the course and done your duty.
So, I will give you your heaven; whatever you want it to be
Come tomorrow and reveal your heaven to me."
My heaven? My goodness, what would it be?

Surround myself with my loving family?
That doesn't make sense to me.
What age would they be?
Besides there are some, I don't care to see!

Let my soul drift in a cloud for an eternity of bliss?
That wouldn't work for me; think what all I would miss!

Stand on the tee at the Masters with fifty thousand people,
National TV, Tiger Woods and me.
Not that!
Glory is short lived and there I'd be!

Give me a million dollars and let me go on a buying spree.
Then I remember money can buy anything,
But health and happiness; sometimes misery.

Then I drifted off in a very deep sleep.
When I awakened, my idea for my heaven came to me.
This is what I want my heaven to be…

Where I can walk in the lilies by a mountain stream,
Where I can watch the fish swim and play,

Hear the birds sing their songs and see the trees swing and sway.

Listen to the waterfalls and see the mountains reaching up to the sky
Look up in the night and watch the stars go by –
The quietness of night that reminds us, we are not alone.

Where people rise early on a foggy morning to witness the muted pink
and purple sunrise
Struggling to break through the magical theatre of God.

Where the bears roam at night and hummingbirds swarm in the day
To hear your friend call and say, "Let's play, let's play!"

To hear the crackling of a hickory wood fire on a bitter cold night,
Snow glistening on the ground under the light of a full moon,
what a wonderful sight,
Fried chicken on a Sunday night,
Dancing to "Sweet Caroline" with Banks and Shane makes
everything seem so right.

Oh God, this is my heaven, and don't you dally – send me back to
Sapphire Valley.

Epilogue

Wiley said his life had been fun, challenging, rewarding and filled with interesting and wonderful family and friends. He earned respect in both the business and social world. Throughout his life, he was blessed with excellent health due in large part to good diet and exercise.

I consider myself lucky to be part of Wiley's family. As a father, he led by example. As a friend, he was always there when I called upon him. And as a community leader, he touched and brightened many lives. I will always cherish our time together.

God bless you, Wiley Virden, and thank you for your love, honesty and your relentless dedication to making the world a better place.

Scott Graham

Country Club of Sapphie Valley - 1998

Books about Wiley W. Virden, Jr.

To obtain copies of
From Possum to Caviar
The Life and Times of Wiley Walter Virden
Contact author Scott Graham
Email: wsgt@bellsouth.net

404.431.2560

400 Lees Trace, Marietta, GA 30064

To obtain copies of
Survivor of T-Bone Hill.
MSG Wiley W. Virden
Contact author Norm Cooper
Appalachian Books
P. O. Box 2814
Blairsville, Georgia
Email: abp.georgia@outlook.com
Text or Call - 706.400.1461